D1365783

CALGARY PUBLIC LIBRARY

MANITOBA

GLORIOSUS · ET · LIBER

HARRY BECKETT

Weigl

CALGARY

www.weigl.com

Published by Weigl Educational Publishers Limited
6325 – 10 Street SE
Calgary, Alberta
Canada T2H 2Z9
Web site: http://www.weigl.com
Copyright © 2001 WEIGL EDUCATIONAL PUBLISHERS LIMITED
All rights reserved. No part of this publication may be reproduced, stored in a
retrieval system, or transmitted in any form or by any means, electronic, mechanical,
photocopying, recording, or otherwise, without the prior written permission of Weigl
Educational Publishers Limited.

Canadian Cataloguing in Publication Data
Beckett, Harry, 1936-
 Manitoba

 (Eye on Canada)
 Includes Index
 ISBN 1-896990-79-7

 1. Manitoba--Juvenile literature. I. Title. II. Series:
FC3661.2.B43 2000   j971.27   C00-911112-3
F1062.4.B43 2000

Printed and bound in the United States
1 2 3 4 5 6 7 8 9 0   05 04 03 02 01

We acknowledge the
financial support of
the Government of
Canada through the
Book Publishing
Industry Development
Program (BPIDP) for
our publishing activities.

Photograph Credits

Every reasonable effort has been made to trace ownership and to obtain permission to
reprint copyright material. The publishers would be pleased to have any errors or
omissions brought to their attention so that they may be corrected in subsequent
printings.

Barrett and Mackay: pages cover 13M, 21B, 27M-R; Sandy Black: page 7M; Canadian
Broadcasting Corporation: page 24T-R; Corel Corporation: pages 6T-R, 11, 16B-R,
22T-R, 26B-R, 27T-L; Doug Dealy Photographic Service: pages 4, 5L, 6B, 7B, 8,
10B-L, 12B-L, 13T-L, 14, 15B-L, 15M-R, 27B-L; Festival du Voyageur:
page 20T-R; Flin Flon & District Chamber of Commerce: page 7T-L; Folklorama,
Folk Arts Council of Winnipeg Inc.: page 23B-R; Geovisuals: page 13B; Gimli
Icelandic Festival: page 20B; Glenbow Archives: page 17T-L (NA17-12); Hoover
Photography ©: page 23T-L; Hudson Bay Company Archives, Provincial Archives
of Manitoba: pages 16T-L (HBCA P-417), 17B-L (HBCA P-392 (N13494)),
18B (HBCA P-378 (N87-8)); Inco Limited: pages 3T-R, 9B; International Peace
Garden: page 23B; Keith Levit Photography: page 26T; © M. Macri/Sea North Tours:
page 12B-R; Manitoba Hydro: page 9T-L; Mennonite Heritage Village Museum:
page 22M-L, 22B; National Archives of Canada: pages 3M-R (PA27942), 17B-R
(C6896), 18T-R (C46091), 19M-L (PA27942),19B (C6623); Norihiko Onishi/Aurora
Domes, Churchill Manitoba: page 10T-R; Parks Canada: page 24B-R; Provincial
Archives of Manitoba: pages 19T-R (CN45), 21L (C93-184); Province of Manitoba:
page 1; Reuters/Tami Chappell/Archive Photos: pages 24B-L; Thompson Festival
of the Arts: pages 3B-R, 25B-L; Winnipeg Fringe Theatre Festival: page 25T-R.

Project Coordinator
Jill Foran
Design
Lucinda Cage
Warren Clark
Copy Editor
Heather Kissock
Layout
Lucinda Cage
Cover Design
Terry Paulhus
Photo Researcher
Alan Tong

CONTENTS

INTRODUCTION

Manitoba is the easternmost of the three Prairie Provinces. The other two provinces are Saskatchewan, its western neighbour, and Alberta. Ontario lies to the east of Manitoba, and Nunavut lies to the north. North Dakota borders Manitoba's southwest, and Minnesota borders the southeast.

Manitoba is known as Canada's Keystone Province. A keystone is the stone at the top of an arch that balances the weight of both sides, keeping the arch in place. Manitoba balances eastern and western Canada. It lies in the centre of the country, a transportation **junction** between the industrial centres of the east and the prairies and mountains of the west.

Manitoba's southern region is a major contributor to Canada's breadbasket. Vast harvests of wheat, barley, oats, and flax come out of the region.

QUICK FACTS

Winnipeg is the capital of Manitoba.

Manitoba's provincial motto is "Gloriosus et Liber," which means "Glorious and free."

The prairie crocus is the provincial flower of Manitoba.

The white spruce is the provincial tree of Manitoba.

There are many ways to get to the centre of Canada. Major airlines fly to Winnipeg International Airport, and other towns in the province have airstrips that smaller aircraft can use.

The major highway across Manitoba is the Trans-Canada Highway. It cuts through the southern part of the province, in an east–west direction. Another important highway is the Yellowhead Route, which runs further north, but almost parallel to the Trans-Canada Highway. To get to northern Manitoba, drivers can take one of two highways. Highway 6 runs from Winnipeg to Thompson, and Highway 10 runs from Dauphin to Flin Flon. Most of the major routes meet in Winnipeg.

The train is another way to get to Manitoba. Canada's passenger train, Via Rail, serves Winnipeg and many of the province's smaller communities.

Winnipeg is the oldest city in the Prairies.

In winter, the province's frozen lakes can be used as roads to bring goods to the isolated northern communities.

The northern communities of Manitoba do not have good road or rail links, but most are served by local airlines.

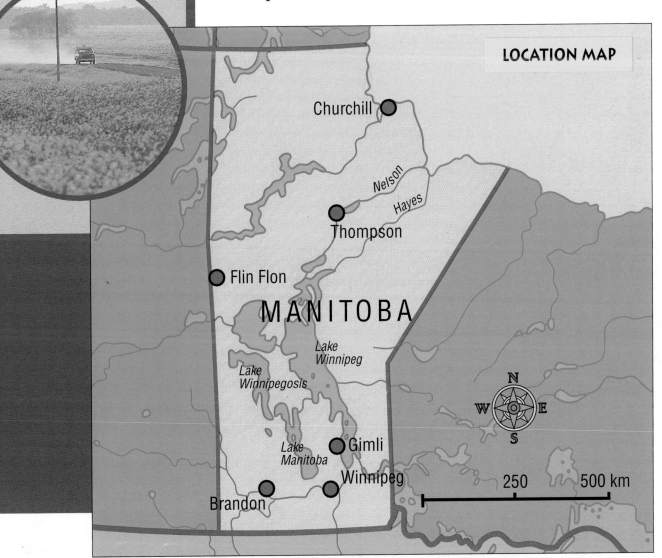

LOCATION MAP

Churchill

Nelson

Hayes

Thompson

Flin Flon

MANITOBA

Lake Winnipeg

Lake Winnipegosis

N
W   E
S

Lake Manitoba

Gimli

Winnipeg

250   500 km

Brandon

Although Manitoba is known as a Prairie Province, its natural scenery extends beyond flat, treeless landscapes. Rocky terrains, small mountains, and dense forest regions can all be found in the province.

Manitoba also has lakes. In fact, it has about 100,000 of them. These lakes are the remains of a huge body of water known as Lake Agassiz, which covered the southern region after the Ice Age. Today, Manitoba's largest lakes are Lake Winnipeg, Lake Winnipegosis, and Lake Manitoba. Rivers in Manitoba include the Saskatchewan, Red, Nelson, Churchill, and Assiniboine rivers and their **tributaries**. About 25 percent of North America's fresh water drains through Manitoba's rivers into Hudson Bay.

Lake Winnipeg is the sixth largest lake in Canada. Throughout history, it has served as a waterway for fur traders, a reserve for fishers, a source of hydroelectricity, and a great location for watersports.

QUICK FACTS

Lake Winnipeg has an area of 24,514 square kilometres, making it the thirteenth largest lake in the world.

Although it is in the heart of Canada, Manitoba has more than 600 km of salt water coastline. A part of Northern Manitoba runs along the shore of Hudson Bay.

The city of Flin Flon may have been named for Professor Josiah Flintabbatey Flonatin, a character in a science fiction novel titled *The Sunless City* by E. Preston Muddock.

When Manitoba joined Confederation in 1870, it was a small, square area—36,000 sq km—surrounding the Red River Valley. The province was enlarged in 1881 and again in 1912 to its present area of 649,950 sq km.

Winnipeg is sixteen times as big as the next largest Manitoba city, Brandon.

The name Manitoba probably comes from the Algonquian words "Manitou bau," which mean "Strait of the Spirit," or "Narrows of the Great Spirit." The name refers to a narrow part of Lake Manitoba. When the lake's waves break on the loose surface rocks of the north shore, they make an odd wailing sound. Early Native peoples thought this was the sound of the Great Spirit Manitou beating on a huge drum.

Manitoba has a number of unique cities and communities. Winnipeg is the largest city in the province. It is the centre of road, rail, and river networks. Other Manitoba communities include Brandon and Portage-la-Prairie, both of which lie west of Winnipeg, Flin Flon, which lies northwest of Winnipeg, and Thompson, in the far north. Churchill is even farther north, nestled on the shores of the Hudson Bay.

Brandon is nicknamed the "Wheat City" because of its strong agricultural heritage and successful farming communities.

Winnipeg is located at the junction of the Red and Assiniboine rivers.

LAND AND CLIMATE

Manitoba's southern region consists of plains with rolling grasslands and few trees. However, prairie does not dominate the entire Manitoba landscape. North of Winnipeg, the prairie gives way to sparkling lakes and dense forests.

The **Canadian Shield** is another feature of Manitoba's landscape. It makes up about two thirds of the province's northern region, and consists mainly of low hills, forests, lakes, and a plateau of soft rock from ancient mountains. To the far north, stretching about 160 km inland from Hudson Bay, is the Hudson Bay Lowland. It is a cold, treeless area of **tundra.**

Warm, moist ocean winds do not reach Manitoba because it is 2,000 km from the Pacific Ocean. The province's location results in long, cold winters, and warm, short summers. The climate is quite dry, and most precipitation falls in the summer as short bursts of rain. Snowfall in Manitoba is not heavy, but due to the cold winter temperatures, snow stays on the ground from November to April.

The large, ancient rocks of the Canadian Shield are often marked with coloured streaks and deposits of minerals. Some of these rocks are almost as old as the Earth itself.

QUICK FACTS

There is a hilly region in the southwest of Manitoba. Highlands in this region are called The Porcupine Hills, the Duck Mountains, and the Turtle Mountains. The Turtle Mountains are the lowest mountain range in North America.

Mount Baldy, in the Duck Mountains, is the province's highest point.

Gravel beaches and sandy delta areas on the Manitoba plains show the former shore-line of Lake Agassiz.

Most of the land in Manitoba is very flat, and flooding and erosion are always a threat. Many farmers have planted trees around their properties to act as windbreaks. They have also dug irrigation ditches to funnel away flood waters.

The province's extra hydroelectric power is sold to other provinces.

Half of Manitoba is covered with non-productive forest. This means the trees are not suitable for the lumber industry.

One of Manitoba's most valuable resources is its fertile prairie land. About 7.6 million hectares of this land are used for farming.

NATURAL RESOURCES

Manitoba's waters are an important resource. Not only are they well suited to recreational activities, they also contain fish that support both commercial and sport fishing. The province's swift-flowing rivers are excellent for the production of **hydroelectric power**. The production is so efficient that Manitoba provides more electricity than it needs from its hydroelectric power plants.

Manitoba also has many useful minerals. The Canadian Shield contains large amounts of metallic **ores**. The most important is nickel, which makes up 30 percent of the value of all the minerals mined in the province. All the nickel is produced in the northern city of Thompson. Flin Flon is the oldest of the mining centres and produces copper, zinc, and small amounts of gold and silver. Precious metals have also been found at centres such as Lynn Lake and Leaf Rapids. Petroleum is another important natural resource in Manitoba. It is found in the area of Virden, in the southwest region of the province.

Smelting involves melting ore in order to obtain metal. This smelter, located in Thompson, produces nickel.

PLANTS AND ANIMALS

The vegetation in Manitoba is diverse. Tall, mixed grass species make up most of the southern prairie area. Willows, aspens, and poplars grow in the moist river valleys, and some oaks grow in dry spots. From spring to fall, wildflowers appear among the grasses. Further north, there are regions of open prairie with stands of aspen, birch, and poplar. Still further north, the forests are a mixture of **coniferous** and **deciduous** trees.

There are also colourful chokecherry, cranberry, and saskatoon bushes in Manitoba's wetlands. In the tundra, where the climate is extreme, lichens and mosses cover the ground. Spruce, willows, and bearberry bushes occasionally dot the landscape.

QUICK FACTS

Close to Churchill, the Tundra Aurora Domes are areas with 360° views from which people can watch the northern lights.

Near Hudson Bay, the land is barren and treeless, with a few grasses and wildflowers among the mosses and lichens. Roots are very shallow because the ground is always frozen.

Manitoba has 127 provincial parks, nine natural parks, one wilderness park, thirty-one recreation parks, and many national history parks.

Manitoba's Riding Mountain National Park encompasses vast areas of aspen parkland, deciduous forest, and open grasslands and meadows.

Many types of birds are found in Manitoba. Grouse, wild turkeys, and prairie chickens are common. There are also ducks and geese on the ponds and swamps of the province. Bald eagles are occasionally spotted.

The great grey owl is the provincial bird. It likes to make its home in empty nests in aspen swamps.

Bass, pickerel, pike, sauger, trout, and whitefish are plentiful in Manitoba's lakes and rivers.

Lynxes inhabit Manitoba's northern forests.

Manitoba has an abundance of interesting wildlife. The southern forests are home to moose, caribou, elk, and deer. Black bears, beavers, and other small fur-bearing animals also live in these forests. Wolverines and white and blue foxes live on the tundra, while caribou, wolves, otters, lynx, squirrels, and mink are found in the far north. Coyotes and badgers like Manitoba's open country.

Polar bears can also be seen in Manitoba. A very large community of these bears live near Churchill. Every once in a while, a polar bear will wander into the town attracted by the food in the local garbage dumps. Manitoba's Hudson Bay area also hosts beluga whales. In the summer, hundreds of these whales gather at the mouth of the Churchill River to feed.

Today, there are about 25,000 polar bears in the world. A large number of them can be found in the far north of Manitoba.

TOURISM

Manitoba attracts many wildlife enthusiasts. About 10,000 tourists a year take a ride on a "tundra buggy" from Churchill to watch the polar bears. Other tourists may ride on a **hydrophone**-equipped boat to see and hear the belugas that swim in the area.

The Manitoba Museum of Man and Nature in Winnipeg has several life-size exhibits that show the province's natural and cultural heritage. The Boreal Forest Gallery, for example, depicts Manitoba's most northerly forested region. Other exhibits include pioneer life, a buffalo hunt, and a 1920s Winnipeg street.

Winnipeg is also home to The Forks, a huge riverside area that offers recreational and cultural events to visitors all year round. At the junction of the Red and Assiniboine Rivers, The Forks is a location for concerts, children's programs, historical exhibitions, and shopping. Visitors can hike, ice-skate, or cross-country ski there.

The Forks is one of Winnipeg's most popular gathering places. The market there offers jewellery, crafts, and a variety of fresh and specialty foods.

The belugas that frequent the Hudson Bay draw many tourists to northern Manitoba.

QUICK FACTS

Lower Fort Garry National Historic Site, at Selkirk, still has many of the original buildings from the 1830s Hudson's Bay trading post.

The Royal Canadian Mint, in Winnipeg, makes two billion coins a year for Canada and for many other nations. Thousands of tourists take tours of the factory and museum.

Prairie Dog Central is a steam-driven train that takes tourists on a two-hour, round-trip from Winnipeg to Grosse-Isle.

Grand Beach Provincial Park has white sand beaches that attract many tourists.

The Commonwealth Air Training Plan Museum, in Brandon, is dedicated to the soldiers who fought in the Commonwealth during World War II. It has over 5,000 displays of aircraft memorabilia and artifacts for visitors to enjoy.

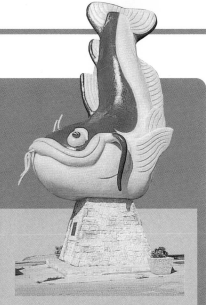

The commercial fishing industry is centred on Manitoba's three major lakes and Hudson Bay. Most of the province's fish is exported to the United States.

Agriculture is confined to the south of the province because the growing season in the north is too short and the soil is poor.

Most of the trees cut in Manitoba are small and are used either to make wood pulp or to build furniture.

Nearly one fifth of Manitoba's wealth comes from financial services, real estate sales, and insurance.

INDUSTRY

Agriculture is one of Manitoba's most important industries. The major crop is wheat. Other significant crops include canola, flaxseed, and barley. Ranching also contributes to the economy.

Manitoba is a vital centre for trade. Winnipeg is one of Canada's leading grain markets. It also trades cattle and serves as a major distribution centre for farm and factory products.

Manufacturing is also important in Manitoba. Processed food, transportation equipment, machinery, and printed products are all manufactured in the province. The most important centre for manufacturing is Winnipeg because of its large supply of inexpensive electricity and its convenient, central location.

Agriculture is the main economic activity for most of the rural communities in southern Manitoba.

Manitoba's railway maintenance facilities and marshalling yards provide many jobs for people in the province.

GOODS AND SERVICES

Manitoba has three universities: the University of Manitoba, the University of Winnipeg, and Brandon University. The University of Manitoba, which is in Winnipeg, is one of the biggest universities in Canada. Community colleges in many Manitoba towns and cities offer training in trades and technologies. Saint Boniface College is located in Winnipeg's French-speaking community of Saint Boniface. The college uses French as its language of instruction.

Not only is Winnipeg the centre of education in the province, it is also the centre of Manitoba's, and Canada's, railway network. To service the engines and train cars, the city has extensive **marshalling yards** and repair facilities.

The University of Manitoba was established in 1877, making it the first university in western Canada.

QUICK FACTS

Winnipeg has ten of Manitoba's eighty hospitals.

There are six daily newspapers in the province and over sixty weekly or bi-weekly newspapers, including *La Liberté*, which is written in French.

Manitoba had the first publicly owned telephone system in North America.

The railway is the most important way of moving goods from Manitoba to other places. Grain is transported by rail to the Atlantic and Pacific oceans and to the port of Churchill on the Hudson Bay. The railway also carries aviation and marine fuels to the Hudson Bay area and minerals from the mines in the Canadian Shield region.

Most highways connect through Winnipeg. Because it is a traffic junction, it is a suitable marketplace for grain, cattle, and farm produce from the Prairies. Many farmers around Winnipeg produce vegetables and dairy goods to sell in the city.

Five television stations and twenty-seven radio stations serve the province.

The shortest route to Europe is via Hudson Bay, but it is not used in winter when the bay is iced over. The alternative route is through the Great Lakes.

The Yellowhead Highway, which passes through Manitoba, roughly follows a part of the Ellice Trail, an old fur-trading route.

The swinging bridge in Souris is 177 metres long. It is the longest swinging bridge in Canada.

Winnipeg has often been regarded as the "Gateway to the West" because of its central location within Canada.

Railway and trucking firms make up the most important part of Manitoba's transportation industry.

FIRST NATIONS

QUICK FACTS

Native groups in the Manitoba region often ended up sharing some hunting and fishing grounds. Sometimes, competition for food and land led to confrontations.

Most historians agree that the first inhabitants arrived in the Manitoba region about 11,000 or 12,000 years ago. These inhabitants were probably **nomadic** hunters who were following the buffalo. Later, Native Peoples began hunting in the northern forests. Early Inuit were on the shores of Hudson Bay about 3,000 years ago.

By the early seventeenth century, five Native groups occupied the Manitoba region. The Inuit lived in the far north, along the Hudson Bay. They hunted whales in the bay and caribou in the forest. Also in the north were the Chipewyans, who competed with the Inuit in hunting for caribou.

The Woodland Cree lived just south of the Inuit and the Chipewyans. This group hunted in the region's rich forest and fished in its rivers. The Ojibway, who were closely related to the Cree, dominated the central Manitoba region. Finally, the Assiniboine lived in the southern region.

Thousands of years ago, Native Peoples may have hunted woolly mammoths in the region.

The Plains Cree fished and trapped animals in the prairies and lowlands of Manitoba.

The Inuit and Chipewyan were natural enemies.

The Assiniboine and Cree were close allies.

Hunting buffalo was an essential part of the Assiniboine's economy and culture.

EXPLORERS

The first European to set foot in the Manitoba region was Captain Thomas Button. He spent the winter of 1612 on the shore of Hudson Bay near the mouths of the Nelson and Hayes rivers. Button claimed the land for Britain. It was many years before other explorers arrived.

In the late 1600s, explorers came looking for furs. The Hudson's Bay Company, a British fur-trading company, built its main post at York Factory on the Hayes River. One of the company's agents, Henry Kelsey, spent three years exploring the area extending from the tundra south to the Saskatchewan River. In the 1730s, a French explorer named Pierre Gaultier de La Vérendrye, led an expedition west from the Great Lakes. He explored the Red River Valley and built four forts.

More French explorers soon followed to set up further posts. Unlicensed French, Scottish, and American trappers also began to operate. The Hudson's Bay Company had always waited for trappers to bring their furs north to them. Now, because of the new competition, the company had to start building posts closer to the traders.

Henry Kelsey is famous for exploring the Canadian plains between 1690 and 1692.

Many French fur traders married Cree and Ojibway women. Their children were called Métis.

The Métis learned the skills of both races and were able to help the Europeans survive in harsh conditions.

Thousands of Natives died when Europeans brought diseases such as smallpox to the area.

The English and French competed for control of the fur trade.

La Vérendrye's trading headquarters were at Fort La Reine, near present-day Portage-la-Prairie.

EARLY SETTLERS

During the early 1800s, the Hudson's Bay Company was fighting with the North West Company of Montreal for control of the fur trade. Both companies built forts across the plains and even fought battles in the Red River and Assiniboine River Valleys.

In 1812, Lord Selkirk of the Hudson's Bay Company, sent a group of Scottish immigrants to set up a colony on the Red River. Members of the North West Company, who had forts in the area, saw the move as a plot to block their trading routes. In the spring of 1816, Selkirk's men seized the North West Company's Fort Gibraltar. They were trying to stop the North West Company from exporting **pemmican**. Métis who worked for the North West Company captured the Hudson's Bay Company's Brandon House in order to reclaim the company's pemmican supplies and export them. On June 19, 1816, Governor Robert Semple led a group of settlers out to confront the Métis. What followed was the Seven Oaks Incident. The governor, twenty of Selkirk's men, and one Métis were killed. Peace was restored when the Hudson's Bay Company and the North West Company merged in 1821. Living conditions were hard during the next few years, and the settlers had to learn to live together.

The Seven Oaks Incident was the worst occurrence in a long rivalry between the Hudson's Bay Company and the North West Company.

QUICK FACTS

Missionaries arrived in Manitoba around the same time as the first settlers.

Winnipeg grew around Fort Garry, one of the chief centres of the Hudson's Bay Company, in the 1800s.

Missionaries were the first people to build schools in Manitoba. Joseph Provencher opened the first school in 1818, and John West opened another school two years later.

Manitoba's settlers survived many hardships before farming became established in the Red River Valley.

About 125,000 immigrants arrived from eastern Canada, Britain, and Europe between 1871 and 1891.

German-speaking Mennonites came to Manitoba from Russia, fleeing from war and violence. They set up the first Mennonite Brethren Congregation near Winkler.

In 1896, the government sent Clifford Sifton on a campaign to Eastern Europe to offer free land to peasant farmers. About 200,000 immigrants arrived in a period of fifteen years.

Louis Riel (centre) was the head of a provisional government that negotiated the terms of Manitoba's formation.

The Canadian government bought the whole northwest of Canada from the Hudson's Bay Company in 1869. The Métis were angry that the deal had been done without their being consulted. Led by Louis Riel, they set up their own government and fought against the transfer of the Red River Valley to Canada. The Canadian government and the Métis reached an agreement a year later with the Manitoba Act. This act made Manitoba the fifth province of Canada and provided a Bill of Rights for the Métis. The bill included French Roman Catholic Schools for the Métis and the official use of the French language.

Manitoba's population increased rapidly after it became a province and the railroad reached the region. The fertile prairies and the demand for wheat attracted settlers from eastern Canada and immigrants from all over Europe.

Advertisements brought thousands of settlers to the Manitoba region.

POPULATION

Manitoba has a population of 1.1 million. The province is made up of many cultures. People have come from all over the world to make their homes in Manitoba.

The towns and villages of the southwest, where Lord Selkirk's colonists once settled, are mainly British, while people with French ancestry live mostly south of Winnipeg.

In 1881, the Canadian Pacific Railway reached Winnipeg. Many of the Chinese workers who built the railway decided to make their home in Manitoba. Their descendants are still there today. In 1896, when the Canadian government offered inexpensive land to Europeans, many took up the offer. Icelanders set up a fishing and farming community near Gimli. Today, Gimli is a thriving Icelandic community.

After World War I, the only large wave of immigrants to arrive in Manitoba consisted of Hutterites from the United States who moved to the province in 1918, but thousands of refugees arrived from war-torn Europe after World War II.

The community of Gimli, on the west shore of Lake Winnipeg, is the largest Icelandic settlement outside of Iceland.

QUICK FACTS

Manitoba has one of the largest French populations west of Quebec.

Only 5 percent of Manitoba's population live in the northern and eastern parts of the province.

Native Peoples make up about 12 percent of Manitoba's population.

In the last thirty years, many of Manitoba's immigrants have come from the Caribbean, Central and South America, Africa, and Asia.

POLITICS AND GOVERNMENT

Manitoba became a Canadian province on July 15, 1870. The first provincial government had twenty-four members, twelve each from English and French districts. Today, the Legislative Assembly has fifty-seven elected members (MLAs) in one chamber. The majority party forms the government, and its leader, the premier, chooses a Cabinet. This executive council decides on government policy and carries out the Assembly's decisions.

Municipalities are responsible for local services such as roads and sewers. Community councils, mainly Métis, give advice to the Department of Northern Affairs in the smaller northern areas. Provincial policing is provided by the Royal Canadian Mounted Police, though cities and towns employ a number of police officers to maintain law and order.

In 1911, an architectural contest was held to see who could come up with the best design for the province's Legislative Building. An architect named Frank Worthington Simon won the contest, and the $10,000 prize.

Manitoba has fourteen federal members of Parliament and six senators.

Yvon Dumont was appointed the first Métis Lieutenant Governor of Manitoba in 1993.

Edward Richard Schreyer, a Manitoban, was the youngest MLA ever. He entered the legislature at the age of twenty-two and became premier of Manitoba at thirty-three. He later became the governor general of Canada.

The first seven governments in Manitoba were non-partisan, meaning they had no distinct political parties.

CULTURAL GROUPS

Manitoba has more ethnic groups than any other province. These groups are proud of their various heritages and work hard to maintain and celebrate their cultural traditions. Many of the Icelanders who settled on the southern shore of Lake Winnipeg have kept their language and customs alive. Every year, they share their culture with others at Islendingadagurinn, or the Gimli Icelandic Festival.

Many descendants of Manitoba's original Mennonite settlers have retained the old culture and traditions. The Mennonite Heritage Village in Steinbach gives visitors an idea of what an original Mennonite village looked like. Antiques, manuscripts, furnished buildings, and a **gristmill** are all part of the village.

QUICK FACTS

About 74 percent of Manitobans have English as their first language.

Most of Manitoba's Native Peoples speak English, but Cree, Chipewyan, and Sioux are also heard around the province.

Rodeos in Manitoba celebrate the province's cattle ranching roots.

The other major languages spoken in the province are French, German, and Ukrainian. These languages are mainly spoken in rural communities.

The Mennonite Heritage Village has a gristmill and a windmill. Mennonites brought their knowledge of mills from countries such as Belgium, Germany, and the Netherlands.

Dauphin, in southwest Manitoba, holds the annual Canadian National Ukrainian Festival every summer.

The Red River Exhibition, held for ten days in June, celebrates Winnipeg's history.

The Jewish community in Manitoba is very strong. It has raised millions of dollars to build the Asper Jewish Community Centre, which houses a high school, a modern fitness centre, and community groups.

Saint Boniface is a strong francophone community. Every February, the community honours the early fur traders at the Festival du Voyageur. **Tourtière** and sugar pie, dishes the voyagers would have enjoyed, are among the traditional foods served during the festival.

One of Manitoba's most important festivals is Folklorama. This festival of nations takes place every August and features more than thirty-five **pavillions** that exhibit and celebrate ethnic cultures. There, Manitoba's various cultural groups share their traditions with other Manitobans and with visitors. Traditional food, dancing, music, costumes, and crafts are all a part of the festival.

The International Peace Garden is another source of cultural celebration. On the border with the United States, the International Peace Garden honours the relationship between Canada and the United States. Every summer, students from all over North America travel there to attend an International Music Camp for band, choir, orchestra, dance, and drama.

Folklorama showcases the talents of various cultural groups that live in Manitoba.

The Peace Tower at the International Peace Garden has four columns representing the four corners of the world.

ARTS AND ENTERTAINMENT

Manitoba has a strong music scene, ranging from country music festivals to a highly praised symphony orchestra. Music festivals throughout the province offer great entertainment. The Winnipeg Folk Festival attracts singers and musicians from all over North America. Other festivals include The International Old-time Fiddle Contest at the International Peace Gardens, the Cripple Creek Music Festival of Bluegrass, Country, and Gospel music, the Brandon Folk Music and Art Festival, and the Classic Rock Weekend at Minnedosa.

Manitobans have done well in rock and pop music. The Crash Test Dummies, Burton Cummings and Randy Bachman of The Guess Who, and Chantal Kreviazuk are all world-famous performers who hail from Manitoba.

QUICK FACTS

Fred Penner, a famous children's entertainer, is from Manitoba.

The Winnipeg Symphony and the Winnipeg Chamber Orchestra are respected throughout Canada.

During the 1930s, conservation writer Grey Owl lived in Riding Mountain National Park.

Chantal Kreviazuk is from Winnipeg. Her music is popular in Canada and around the world.

The Winnipeg Art Gallery has a huge display of Inuit artwork.

Two of Manitoba's best-known authors are Margaret Laurence and Gabrielle Roy. Many of their novels are about Manitoba life.

The Cercle Molière in Saint Boniface is one of the oldest French language theatres in the country.

The Saint Boniface Museum dates from 1846 and is the oldest building in Winnipeg. It is also the largest oak log Red River Frame building in North America.

The Winnipeg Fringe Festival provides live theatre in an informal setting. It is one of the largest Fringe Festivals in North America.

Manitoba is rich in other art forms as well. The Royal Winnipeg Ballet, which was founded in 1938, is the second oldest ballet company in North America. It has performed all over the world.

Each summer, Rainbow Stage puts on two Broadway musicals in Winnipeg's Kildonan Park. The Manitoba Theatre Centre has a main stage where it presents a series of well-known plays. Less **mainstream** productions take place on the centre's smaller stage. The Fringe Festival puts on plays and revues written mostly by Manitobans.

Many talented artists and architects are from Manitoba. Lionel Fitzgerald was a member of the famous **Group of Seven**. Walter Phillips is a Manitoban whose etchings, woodcuts, and prints are very popular. Important Manitoban architects have also made an impact on the art world. John D. Atchison designed nearly one hundred of the buildings in Winnipeg, and Étienne Gaboury has designed important buildings in Saint Boniface, Mexico, and Africa.

Dancers from all over Canada work hard for the opportunity to dance with the Royal Winnipeg Ballet.

SPORTS

The 1999 Pan-American Games were held in Winnipeg. The games attracted over 5,000 athletes from forty-two countries.

Sports such as hockey, ringette, and curling are all very popular in Manitoba because of its long, cold winters. There are leagues for every age group. The Winnipeg Jets was Manitoba's professional hockey team. The Jets played in the World Hockey Association until 1979, at which time they became a part of the National Hockey League. In 1997, they moved to Phoenix, Arizona and became the Phoenix Coyotes.

Winnipeg hosted the Pan-American Games in 1967 and again in 1999. Excellent facilities were built for the games. Today, Winnipeg has an Olympic-sized swimming pool, which also houses the Aquatic Hall of Fame. It also has an indoor cycling track, a stadium, a track facility, and a rifle range. They are used by Manitoba's top athletes and by the general public for recreation.

QUICK FACTS

Manitoba has produced many hockey stars. Bobby Clarke is from Flin Flon, Reggie Leach from Riverton, and Bill Mosienko and Terry Sawchuk from Winnipeg. Bill Ranford, Ed Belfour, and Ken Wregget are others who have made their mark in the NHL.

In 1981, Vicki Keith, from Winnipeg, swam across all five Great Lakes.

The Winnipeg Blue Bombers are a team in the Canadian Football League.

Manitoba has more golf courses per head than any other province.

The Manitoba Curling Association Bonspiel is one of the world's biggest curling competitions.

Manitoban Sylvia Burka competed internationally in two sports—speed skating and cycling. She won five national skating titles in the 1970s, and set a world record in cycling in 1982.

The National Frog Jumping Championships are the highlight of Saint Pierre's Frog Follies.

The World Championship Dog Sled races take place at the Northern Manitoba Trappers' Festival in The Pas.

Manitoba has many provincial parks that have wonderful facilities for skiers, hikers, campers, backpackers, tennis players, and lawn bowlers. Lovers of water sports can swim, sail, water ski, and scuba dive at places such as Falcon Lake in Whiteshell Provincial Park, and Clear Lake in Riding Mountain National Park. Anyone interested in fishing can take part in Flin Flon's Trout Festival.

Riding Mountain National Park is home to wildlife such as black bear, moose, elk, deer, wolves, and bison. It is on a wooded section of the Manitoba **Escarpment**, 744 metres above the prairie. The escarpment has thirty-six hiking and riding trails through gorges, lakes, forests, and bogs. It also has golf facilities.

Whiteshell Provincial Park has over 130 lakes that are great for fishing, boating, or swimming.

Winnipeg Beach is one of many beaches that Manitoba has to offer.

EYE ON CANADA

Manitoba is one of the ten provinces and three territories that make up Canada. Compare Manitoba's statistics with those of other provinces and territories. What differences and similarities can you find?

Northwest Territories

Entered Confederation:
July 15, 1870

Capital: Yellowknife

Area: 171,918 sq km

Population: 41,606
Rural: 58 percent
Urban: 42 percent

Population Density:
0.24 people per sq km

Yukon

Entered Confederation:
June 13, 1898

Capital: Whitehorse

Area: 483,450 sq km

Population: 30,633
Rural: 40 percent
Urban: 60 percent

Population Density:
0.06 people
per sq km

British Columbia

Entered Confederation:
July 20, 1871

Capital: Victoria

Area: 947,800 sq km

Population: 4,023,100
Rural: 18 percent
Urban: 82 percent

Population Density:
4.24 people
per sq km

Alberta

Entered Confederation:
September 1, 1905

Capital: Edmonton

Area: 661,190 sq km

Population: 2,964,689
Rural: 20 percent
Urban: 80 percent

Population Density:
4.48 people
per sq km

Saskatchewan

Entered Confederation:
September 1, 1905

Capital: Regina

Area: 652,330 sq km

Population: 1,027,780
Rural: 28 percent
Urban: 72 percent

Population Density:
1.57 people per sq km

Manitoba

Entered Confederation:
July 15, 1870

Capital: Winnipeg

Area: 649,950 square km

Population: 1,143,509
Rural: 28 percent
Urban: 72 percent

Population Density:
1.76 people per sq km

250   500 km

Nunavut

Entered Confederation:
April 1, 1999

Capital: Iqaluit

Area: 1,900,000 sq km

Population: 27,039

Population Density:
0.014 people per sq km

Quebec

Entered Confederation:
July 1, 1867

Capital: Quebec City

Area: 1,540,680 sq km

Population: 7,345,390
Rural: 21 percent
Urban: 79 percent

Population Density:
4.77 people per sq km

CANADA

Confederation:
July 1,1867

Capital: Ottawa

Area: 9,203,054 sq km

Population: 30,491,294
Rural: 22 percent
Urban: 78 percent

Population Density:
3.06 people
per sq km

Newfoundland & Labrador

Entered Confederation:
March 31, 1949

Capital: St. John's

Area: 405,720 sq km

Population: 541,000
Rural: 43 percent
Urban: 57 percent

Population Density:
1.33 people
per sq km

Prince Edward Island

Entered Confederation:
July 1, 1873

Capital:
Charlottetown

Area: 5,660 sq km

Population: 137,980
Rural: 56 percent
Urban: 44 percent

Population Density:
24.38 people
per sq km

Ontario

Entered Confederation:
July 1, 1867

Capital: Toronto

Area: 1,068,580 sq km

Population: 11,513,808
Rural: 17 percent
Urban: 83 percent

Population Density:
10.77 people per sq km

New Brunswick

Entered Confederation:
July 1, 1867

Capital: Fredericton

Area: 73,440 sq km

Population: 754,969
Rural: 51 percent
Urban: 49 percent

Population Density:
10.28 people per sq km

Nova Scotia

Entered Confederation:
July 1, 1867

Capital: Halifax

Area: 55,490 sq km

Population: 939,791
Rural: 45 percent
Urban: 55 percent

Population Density:
16.94 people
per sq km

BRAIN TEASERS

Test your knowledge of Manitoba by trying to answer these boggling brain teasers!

1 True or False:

A.A. Milne's famous Winnie the Pooh was inspired by a real bear who was named after the city of Winnipeg.

2 Multiple Choice:

Western Canada's oldest opera house is located in

a. Winnipeg.
b. Virden.
c. Flin Flon.
d. Brandon.

3 Multiple Choice:

The word for Gimli means

a. paradise.
b. home.
c. new land.
d. new Iceland.

4 True or False:

The corner of Portage Street and Main Street in Winnipeg has the reputation of being the windiest corner in Canada.

5 True or False:

Eighty percent of the tourists in Manitoba are Manitobans.

6 Make a Guess:

What is the name of the statue that stands on top of Manitoba's Legislative Building?

7 Make a Guess:

Where in Manitoba can exotic animals such as flamingoes, lemurs, and snow leopards be seen?

8 True or False:

Komarno, Manitoba is home to a giant mosquito, with a 4.6 metre wingspan.

1. True. A soldier from Winnipeg bought a bear in Ontario, named it after his home town, and took it to the London Zoo in England, where Milne caught his first glimpse.

2. b. The opera house was built in 1921, and is still in use today.

3. a. Gimli is an Icelandic word meaning "paradise."

4. True.

5. True.

6. The Golden Boy.

7. The zoo at Winnipeg's Assiniboine Park.

8. True. The town has a giant statue of a mosquito that doubles as a weather vane.

GLOSSARY

Canadian Shield: a region of ancient rock that encircles the Hudson Bay and covers part of mainland Canada

coniferous: evergreen trees with needles and cones

deciduous: trees or shrubs that shed leaves every year

escarpment: a steep slope or cliff

gristmill: a mill that grinds grain

Group of Seven: a group of Canadian painters, most famous for their paintings of Canadian landscape

hydroelectric power: the generation of electricity by the power of water

hydrophone: an instrument that detects underwater sounds

junction: a place where railways or other pathways meet

mainstream: the common trend of opinion, art, or activity within a society

marshalling yards: grounds where rail cars are connected and loaded in preparation for transporting goods

nomadic: moving from place to place, looking for food and water

ores: rocks that contain metals

pavillions: buildings that house exhibitions

pemmican: dried meat that is pounded into a paste with melted fat

tourtière: a traditional meat pie, made mainly with pork

tributaries: streams that flow into larger streams or rivers

tundra: an Arctic or subarctic plain with a permanently frozen subsoil where mosses and lichens are the main types of vegetation

BOOKS

Beckett, Harry. *Manitoba*. Florida: The Rourke Book Co., Inc., 1997.

LeVert, Suzanne. *Manitoba*. From the *Let's Discover Canada* series. New York: Chelsea House Publishers, 1991.

Yates, Sarah. *Manitoba*. From the *Hello Canada* series. Minneapolis: Lerner Publishing Groups, 1996.

WEB SITES

Manitoba tourist information
http://travelmanitoba.com

The Government of Manitoba
http://www.gov.mb.ca

Manitoba Museum of Man and Nature
http://www.manitobamuseum.mb.ca

Some Web sites stay current longer than others. To find more Manitoba Web sites, use your Internet search engine to look up such topics as "Manitoba," "Winnipeg," "Prairie Provinces," or any other topic you want to research.

INDEX